Regards from Laura!

The Gift of Love, from God above

A Nativity Play in Rhyme

by

Laura Thompson

© Copyright 2009

All rights reserved. No part of this publication may be
reproduced, stored in a retrieval system, or
transmitted, in any form or by any means,
electronic, mechanical, photocopying, recording
or otherwise, without the prior
written permission of the Publishers.

There is no restriction on the public performance of this play
providing the copyright restrictions as
set out above are adhered to.

British Library Cataloguing in Publication Data.
A catalogue record for this book is available
from the British Library.

If you are unable to purchase sufficient copies for those taking part
you may apply for a Copying Licence from Moorleys.
Schools registered with PLS (Publishers Licensing Society)
can reproduce the script under this Licence providing they record
the Title, Author, Publisher and ISBN on their return.

ISBN 978 086071 627 3

Cover illustration:
Photo © Glenda M. Powers
used under Licence from Shutterstock® Images

23 Park Road, Ilkeston, Derbys DE7 5DA
Tel: 0115 932 0643 www.moorleys.co.uk

The play can be totally mimed, or the words underlined can be spoken

Scene 1

Three kings stand, front left, facing congregation

Narrator
Three kings in Eastern lands afar
Looked up at the sky, as they did every night.
There were lots of stars twinkling down on them,
But one was unusually bright.

What they had seen made their pulses race.
Indeed they were all quite amazed.
A star they had never set eyes on before
In the heavens above brightly blazed.

Now these kings were wise men,
                           and knew straight away
That this star had a message to bring:
That a new baby boy would be born far away,
Not an ordin'ry child, but a king!

They felt in their hearts that this star was their guide
To show them the route they must take.
Before this long journey, through many strange lands,
They had preparations to make.

As well as their stuff, there were presents to pack
For this child of a right royal line,
And destined to be a King of the Jews.
You'd expect them to take something fine.

(Each wise man steps forward as he speaks holding up his gift – words could be taped to top of gift)

The first wise man, so the story goes,
Said, "I'm going to give him gold.
Kings love this more than anything else
In their palaces, so I am told."

The second wise man took a different view:
"Since the new king will be divine,
I'm going to take him frankincense.
I think that will suit him fine."

The third wise man set a sadder tone.
He said, "Kings are mortal and die,
So I will take him a jar of myrrh
To anoint him when his death is nigh."

So now our three kings set off from the East,
With the star to shed comforting light.
They will sleep by day – it's best that way –
And the bright star will guide them by night.

Scene 2

During singing by congregation of 'We Three Kings' (omitting last verse):

Innkeeper stands by the inn (inn to the right)
Mary & Joseph stand in place at left ready to walk to the inn
Animals are in the stable

Angels are hidden (probably in the pulpit if performed in a church)

Narrator
We'll move away now, as they'll take a long time
To reach their ordained destination.
We'll travel through time, to a place far away
And a very important location.

It's Bethlehem city, and full to the brim
With people who've taxes to pay.
Mary and Joseph have made the long trip
And are desperate for somewhere to stay.

They come to an inn, with a sign that says FULL,
And the innkeeper's bolting the door,
When he sees a young woman close to collapse.
So he pokes his head out just once more.

For Mary and Joseph it's the only inn left
And their last hope has faded away.
But the innkeeper, with a rare kindness of heart,
Says they can sleep on the hay.

He's learned that the young girl is soon to give birth,
And he leads them both down to a stable,
With animals just bedding down for the night.
You'd think this whole tale's just a fable!

But no, it is true, and the innkeeper says,
"In here you will be in no danger,
And if your baby should come in the night,
He can sleep, snug and warm, in the manger.

All night the animals stay wide awake
In that lowly cattle stall.
As Jesus is born, the Son of God,
Who has come as a Saviour to all.

(Mary uncovers baby's face in the crib)

Scene 3

Shepherds ready on left side

Narrator
Let the parents and their baby son rest awhile
As we move out of town to a hill,
And into the darkness and frosty night air,
Where some shepherds are feeling the chill.

They are keeping their sheep safe from beasts of prey,
A task they perform every night.
Then all of a sudden the hills are lit up
By a brilliant and dazzling light.

(Angel appears)

An angel appears and calms their great dread,
Saying, "Fear not, my news will bring joy.
In the City of David a Saviour's been born,
Christ the Lord, now a tiny young boy.

Go down there at once to worship this King.
He's not in a grand, royal hall,
But lying, wrapped up in rough bands of cloth,
In a humble cattle stall."

(Rest of angels appear)

The sky then was filled with an angelic host,
Singing praises to God on high,
And blessings of peace to the favoured ones
Resounded throughout the sky.

Scene 4

The shepherds eagerly rushed from the hills
And hastened to Bethlehem,
Where, behind an inn, in a stall, as foretold
(Shepherds move towards stable)
A most wondrous sight greeted them.

The animals knelt, gazing down at the child,
Who lay fast asleep on the hay,
And the shepherds moved up to the makeshift crib
And knelt in a meek, reverent way.

Because they were just humble working men,
Who toiled in the hills every day,
They were never able to worship their God
In the temples where pious men pray.

You might have thought that this message of hope,
This prophesy now become true,
Would hardly concern such men as these,
But Jesus was their Saviour too.

Exit shepherds

Scene 5

Shepherds are sitting down

Narrator
The shepherds return to their work in the hills,
And each night, by the light of their fire,
They'll remember the angel's tidings of joy
And the words of the heavenly choir.

And the young king they'd worshipped that
                                        wonderful night
In a most unexpected, rough place,
And how their humdrum and workaday lives
Were transformed by His heavenly grace.

Scene 6

*Kings get ready to come in left.
Herod goes to stand by palace.*

Some months have now passed since the three kings set out,
And they've come to the land of Judea.
The star is almost overhead now
So they think the new king must be near.

(Kings reach the palace)

They come to a palace, a regal abode,
To inquire if a new prince is here,
As a bright guiding star has led to this place.
At this, Herod is filled with great fear.

He learns that the three kings have come from the East
To search for the King of the Jews.
To Herod, who knows he's omnipotent now,
This comes as the most shocking news.

He is not a good man, but cruel and harsh,
And he's also most terribly wily,
So, while he is planning to kill the young king,
The face that he shows is all smily.

He says, "<u>What splendid news! A new royal prince!
But your star must have led you astray,
For there's no new king here, nor likely to be,
So you'd better all go on your way.</u>"

When they find the young king they must let him know,
As they're passing on their way back,
Since he'd very much like to worship this prince,
And of rich, royal gifts has no lack.

(Kings move towards stable)

The three kings rode on, just a few miles more
Till the star stopped at Bethlehem.
Right over a stable its light shone down,
Which was very puzzling for them.

It was hard to believe that their journey had led
To this poor insignificant stable.
The King they had visited not long before
Had a palace, and sumptuous table!

(Kings reach stable)

They dismounted, and cautiously entered the stall.
Inside, it appeared dark and dim,
But the child was bathed in a heavenly light
And they fell down and worshipped Him.

They unwrapped their frankincense, gold and myrrh,
Those strange, but so apt, gifts they'd brought,
And presented them to the Holy Child
(Place gifts in front of the crib)
The King of the Jews that they'd sought.

(Kings move to the left and rest their cheeks on their hands to simulate sleep)

That night, as they rested, before their return.
At first light on the following day
(Kings wake up – angel appears)
An angel came down to them in a dream,
Saying, "<u>Do not go back the same way,</u>

<u>For Herod is waiting for news of the birth,
Not to worship the child, as he'd said
But to rid himself of this threat to his power
And make sure that his rival is dead."</u>

So the wise men set off for the East once again,
Guided, this time, by the sun.
They would travel by day, to their lands far away,
Much wiser than when they'd begun.

Entire cast come to the front to sing 'Jesus born in a stable bare'.

Narrator
And as our Nativity comes to an end
Let all of us now take a part,
And for God's gift of love, sent from above,
Sing grateful thanks, straight from the heart.

End with suitable carol – suggest 'Love came down at Christmas' by Christina Rossetti

A New Carol for Christmas
Jesus Born in a Stable Bare

Words by Doreen Storr   Music by Joyce Hollingworth

Jesus, born in a stable bare
    Sing, O sing lullaby
Ox and ass were standing near
    Sing, O sing lullaby.

Shepherds came from the fields afar
    Sing, O sing lullaby
Found the babe and Mary there
    Sing, O sing lullaby.

Wise Men followed the shining star
    Sing, O sing lullaby
They brought gifts both rich and rare
    Sing, O sing lullaby.

© Doreen Storr 1985
Originally published in "What shall we do for Christmas?" by Doreen Storr
At time of publication Moorleys have not had any success in contacting Doreen Storr despite starting the process in January 2009

MOORLEYS Print & Publishing

We are growing publishers, adding several new titles to our list each year.
We also undertake private publications and commissioned works.

Our range includes

Books of Verse
Devotional Poetry
Recitations for Children
Humorous Monologues

Drama
Bible Plays
Sketches
Christmas, Passiontide,
Easter and Harvest Plays
Demonstrations

Resource Books
Assembly Material
Easy Use Music Books for Piano and Keyboard
Children's Addresses
Prayers
Worship and Preaching
Books for Speakers

Activity Books
Quizzes
Puzzles

Church Stationery
Notice Books
Cradle Roll Certificates

Associated Lists and Imprints
Cliff College Publishing
Nimbus Press
MET (Headway)
Social Work Christian Fellowship

For up-to-date news, special offers and information on our full list of titles, please visit our website at www.moorleys.co.uk

Alternatively send a stamped addressed C5 envelope for our current catalogue, or consult your local Christian Bookshop, who will either stock or be able to obtain our titles.